Multiply This!

By Melanie Chrismer

Consultant
Ari Ginsburg
Math Curriculum Specialist

Children's Press®
A Division of Scholastic Inc.
New York   Toronto   London   Auckland   Sydney
Mexico City   New Delhi   Hong Kong
Danbury, Connecticut

Designer: Herman Adler Design
Photo Researcher: Caroline Anderson
The photo on the cover shows four cups of three strawberries each,
which equals twelve strawberries in all.

Library of Congress Cataloging-in-Publication Data

Chrismer, Melanie.
  Multiply this! / by Melanie Chrismer ; consultant, Ari Ginsburg.
    p. cm. — (Rookie read-about math)
  Includes index.
  ISBN 0-516-25264-X (lib. bdg.)   0-516-25365-4 (pbk.)
  1. Multiplication—Juvenile literature. I. Ginsburg, Ari. II. Title. III. Series.
  QA115.C465 2005
  513.2'13—dc22   2005004539

CHILDREN'S PRESS, and ROOKIE READ-ABOUT®,
and associated logos are trademarks and/or registered trademarks
of Scholastic Library Publishing. SCHOLASTIC and associated logos
are trademarks and/or registered trademarks of Scholastic Inc.

1 2 3 4 5 6 7 8 9 10 R 14 13 12 11 10 09 08 07 06 05

Tim is hungry.

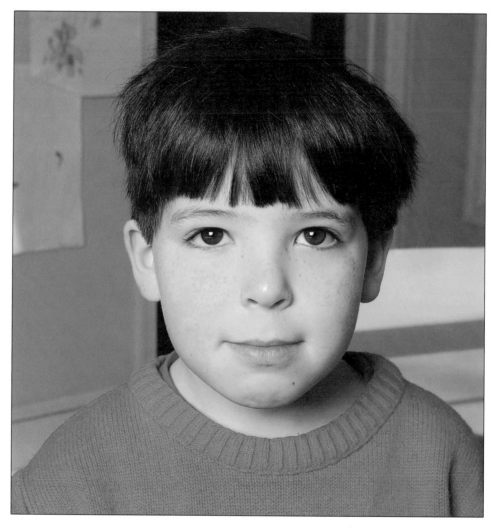

4

He is learning multiplication.
Can he practice his math
as he helps his dad make
breakfast?

Sure! Tim opens the
refrigerator. He sees eggs.

How many eggs does
Tim see?

Tim sees two rows of eggs. Each row has six eggs. How many eggs are there in all?

Tim adds each row of eggs.
6 + 6 = 12
2 groups of 6 = 12

Tim writes: 2 x 6 = 12
The "x" means "groups of."

Two groups of six eggs
equals twelve eggs in all.
Tim just did multiplication!

Tim decides to use the eggs to make pancakes.

He has four people in his family. Each person will want three pancakes.

How many pancakes does Tim need to make? He uses multiplication to find out.

Four groups of three pancakes equals twelve pancakes in all. The answer is twelve!

Multiplication is "fast adding." It is a quick way of adding the same number over and over.

4 x 3 is a different way of figuring out 3 + 3 + 3 + 3.

4 x 3 = 12

Tim and his dad make
sausages next.

Tim's dad cooks two
sausages for each person
in the family.

How many sausages
does he cook in all?

Tim multiplies the number of people by the number of sausages.

Four people times two sausages equals eight sausages in all.

Four groups of two equals eight.

pours the juice. Each
son gets one glass
uice.

many glasses of
does Tim need
pour?

Tir
per
of j

Hc
jui
to

$4 \times 2 =$

4 x 2 = 8

Tim pours the juice. Each person gets one glass of juice.

How many glasses of juice does Tim need to pour?

4 x 1 = 4

Four is the answer!

Tim decides to make
his own multiplication
problems.

He puts refrigerator magnets
in groups.

He makes three groups
of three magnets each.
How many magnets in all?

19

Nine is the answer!

Breakfast is ready.

Dad says, "Please wash
your hands first."

Tim has two hands. He has five fingers on each hand. How many fingers are there in all?

He sees two groups of five fingers.

2 x 5 = 10

Ten is the answer!

Tim is ready to eat. He sees one more multiplication problem.

There are cinnamon rolls for breakfast, too!

In the pan are four rows of four cinnamon rolls each.

How many cinnamon rolls are there in all?

4 x 4 = 16

Sixteen is the answer!

Multiplication is fun and yummy.

Words You Know

cinnamon rolls

eggs

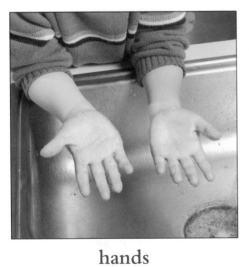

hands

juice

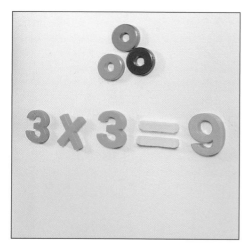

multiplication

pancakes

refrigerator magnets

sausages

31

Index

About the Author

Melanie Chrismer is a writer and flutist who lives near Atlanta, Georgia. She loves reading, writing, and eating yummy cinnamon rolls.

Photo Credits